MW01122248

I, Animal

Also by Daniel MacIvor

Arigato, Tokyo
The Best Brothers
Bingo!
Cul-de-sac
His Greatness
How It Works
In On It
I Still Love You: Five Plays
Marion Bridge
Monster
Never Swim Alone & This Is a Play
One Voice: House and Here Lies Henry
See Bob Run & Wild Abandon
The Soldier Dreams
This Is What Happens Next
Try: Communion, Was Spring, and Small Things
You Are Here

I, Animal
Daniel MacIvor

Playwrights Canada Press
Toronto

I, Animal © 2015 by Daniel MacIvor

For professional or amateur production rights, please contact:
The Gary Goddard Agency
149 Church Street, 2nd Floor
Toronto, ON M5B 1Y4
416-928-0299, meaghan@garygoddardagency.com

Library and Archives Canada Cataloguing in Publication
MacIvor, Daniel, 1962-, author
       I, animal / Daniel MacIvor.

A play.
Contents: Man in scrubs -- Boy in hoodie -- Woman in Prada.
Issued in print and electronic formats.
ISBN 978-1-77091-342-4 (pbk.).--ISBN 978-1-77091-343-1 (pdf).--
ISBN 978-1-77091-344-8 (epub)

       I. Title.

PS8575.I86I12 2015   C812'.54   C2014-908399-8
                                               C2014-908400-5

We acknowledge the financial support of the Canada Council for the Arts, the Ontario Arts Council (OAC), the Ontario Media Development Corporation, and the Government of Canada through the Canada Book Fund for our publishing activities.

 Canada Council for the Arts   Conseil des arts du Canada

 ONTARIO ARTS COUNCIL
CONSEIL DES ARTS DE L'ONTARIO
an Ontario government agency
un organisme du gouvernement de l'Ontario

 Canadä

 Ontario
Ontario Media Development Corporation

For Kat

Introduction

In kabuki theatre there is a gesture called "looking at the moon," and there is a story where an actor—let's call him the first actor—would perform this gesture in a way that made the audience sit up and take notice every time. What beauty in his movements, what feeling, what a masterful actor. And though audiences loved the first actor, the company's teacher was never impressed and felt him not nearly as good as a younger actor in the company—let's call him the second actor—the second actor whom the audience hardly ever noticed. But being a good and gentle man the teacher kept this feeling mostly to himself, realizing it an opinion, not a fact. If the audience was happy, who was the teacher to interfere? One day, a patron of the theatre was singing the praises of the first actor to the teacher, and the teacher gently mentioned his opinion that the second actor was to his eyes superior. The patron was shocked, "Who? I don't even know this actor's name!" The patron went on about the first actor's beautiful hands, the arc of his arm, how his eyes would well with feeling—how could the teacher not offer the first actor the deepest of respect over this invisible second actor? And the teacher said, "When the first actor looks at the moon I see the actor see the moon, when the second actor looks at the moon I see the moon."

I, Animal was written as a Fringe play—first produced by Kazan Co-op at the SuperNova Theatre Festival and then later at SummerWorks in Toronto. I wrote it because I wanted to make something that was first and foremost producible. I've always been a big supporter of the Fringe ideology as a system for cultural entrepreneurs—it seems to be a way for theatre artists to make work and a living at the same time. The idea behind *I, Animal* is that it can be presented as one, two or three monologues and in whatever order one might find efficient or pleasing. Perhaps one actor would play all the parts. I suppose if one wanted to, one might take it apart and use pieces of all three monologues to make an entirely new monologue—something experimental. I'm good with all of that. The premise is simple—its setting is night, outside, under a full moon, and its themes are the things that make us human—or make us question our humanity. Simple. Also, no big design. No fancy soundscape or score. Maybe some pre-show music or songs between monologues—songs you like or songs you think the characters like. Maybe an airplane landing or taking off. A siren. A dog barking. Things you might hear at night outside. Simple. No big lighting set-up. One light or two lights and some fill. (Or do it outside under a street light or in a parking lot on a full moon.) No props are required other than a leash, a suitcase, a phone and a flashlight. Simple simple simple. It's not about the design. Actually it's not even really about the text. It's all about the performances. These are not director's pieces. There's no big mystery, no underlying message, nothing to be decoded, no concept to be discovered. If you're a director reading this looking for something to put your conceptual stamp on—look elsewhere. These are pieces for performers. A director should be assisting as long as that assistance is to discover authenticity in performance. As performers, pull the pieces apart and put them back together, find your place in these characters and these characters in you. There is a spot where it's all the same thing. Find that. The audience should walk away from *I, Animal* carrying the performances—not the ideas or the pretty words—and if it all goes well, maybe the moon.

Daniel MacIvor
March 2015
Avondale, Nova Scotia

I, Animal was first produced by Kazan Co-op in May 2012 at Neptune Theatre, Halifax, Nova Scotia, as part of the SuperNova Theatre Festival. It featured the following cast and creative crew:

Man In Scrubs: Antonio Cayonne
Boy In Hoodie: Stewart Legere
Woman In Prada: Kathryn MacLellan

Director: Richie Wilcox
Light design: Ingrid Risk
Costume design: Janet MacLellan
Set design: Victoria Marsten
Sound design and composition: Aaron Collier

Man In Scrubs

Night. A dog park.

A black man in scrubs carries a leash.

(off) Larry. Larry. Larry! Good!

(to us) They said I had no business going off like that. They said I had no reason to be offended.

(off) Larry.

(to us) They said I had no right.

(off) Larry!

(to us) But how do they know that. They don't know me.

(off) Good!

(to us) But I gotta be what I am. Believe what I am.

Be what I believe.

   He watches off after his dog a moment.

I'm on staff. We work together. We've got to be able to work together. He's a doctor. Yeah yeah. That's a big deal. That's a great divide. It's not like on TV. The doctors and the nurses being at the same parties, arguing in the hallways of the hospital, going out to lunch together in expensive restaurants. You're not going to see that in real life. But that's why there's TV. A nurse hanging out with a doctor. It'd be like hanging out with your landlord. It'd be like going out with your landlord if you lived in a building of over a hundred units. That's what it's like. Because that's what we do. We just rent the patients. The patients belong to the doctor.

How many people ever go out with their landlord to a fancy restaurant? Unless you live with your landlord. Or are a landlord. And sometimes you rent a place and you don't pay much attention to it; and sometimes you rent a place and you paint and put in new floors and install a washer and a dryer. That can happen. People do that. I'd do that if I had the cash. I've always preferred renting. Who owns anything? Tee used to say "leave the campsite better than how you found it." I always remembered that. I built my life around that. Since Tee.

(off) Larry!

(to us) So he is trying to tell me what I can or can't say? How I may or may not identify myself. That's bullshit.

He looks off after his dog.

I've got a temper. I got it from my old man. People always said "you got your temper from your father." And everybody knows the best way to pass on a temper. *Whack.* I should put that in a book. That's what I'd call it. *Whack.*

(off) Larry!

(to us) People treat their dogs better than they treat their people.

That's one crazy dog. I mean he's a great dog. But he sure is horny. That's a dog who loves dogs. Most people don't care. Most people think it's funny. Some people freak out. Some dogs freak out. Some dogs love it.

(off) Larry! No! Sorry about that. Not to worry, he's been fixed. He's shooting blanks.

He makes a shooting gesture.

(to us) He's not loaded. But he sure still gets cocked.

He watches off after the person he was speaking to. He turns to us.

The lady keeps looking back. Her purse all up on her and carrying her little dog. Let's say she's deaf. In that outfit she could be blind and deaf. Let's say she's deaf as a bag of leaves and now she's on her way to the police to tell them there was a "suspicious-looking man in the park and he began making shooting gestures at my dog and I." She might. Stranger things have happened. Far stranger.

(off) Larry!

(to us) Most people don't care. Most people know Larry. It's the breeders. When Larry comes at their dogs with his humping the breeders go nuts. It's not sex—he's got no balls—it's not sex, it's dominance. That's the kind of animal Larry is. The breeders are like that with all the dogs. Come near them and it's like they can see their bank account draining. All you have to do is look and see he's got no balls. But the breeders don't look too closely at mutts like Larry. I say don't come to the park if you're a breeder. I say no breeders allowed. *(laughs)* I should give that to the Pride Day people. For the posters. "No Breeders Allowed!" And no offence intended, okay? Just I preferred things back when we were over the rainbow and under the radar. Yeah, yeah, I believe that we're all one world and all that. But that *human race* idea doesn't take into account personalities. And everybody's got one and they're all different. And you can't get rid of it ever. Even in a mirror. You can't stare it out of yourself. I've tried. I mean you can alter it and all that. Join a group or take a pill. But you've always got that "you" to contend with. This personality. I'll say about personalities, I'll

say eighty percent of the people are assholes and twenty percent of the people are angels. And I mean no religious implications there. I mean people with no ego and who help people and don't think about what they get out of it. An angel. They're rare. Even those angels on American TV who go around and give people second chances are only doing it because of the guy with the book. Because of the judge.

(off) Larry.

(to us) Tee used to say everybody has some good in them. That every person is each an eighty percent asshole and a twenty percent angel. But I have not in my own experience found that to be true. My personality has come up against a lot of hardcore assholes. *(laughing)* Oh I hear Tee now. Uh huh uh huh.

He looks off at the dog a moment.

So somebody says there's a get-together. But there's no sign for the get-together because apparently nobody could agree on what the sign would say. That should have been a hint. And first the get-together is in the cafeteria and then it's in the pub around the corner and then it's at some restaurant. I've been there before for drinks. I wouldn't eat there. My mother boiled water full time for fifty years and she would die twice for what they charge for a plate of spaghetti. I mean I've got a lifestyle to maintain. I've got rent to pay. I've got a hungry dog to feed.

(off) Larry.

(to us) So I go to the damn restaurant. And I feel all this pressure to eat because everybody's eating. And they're all ordering wine. And I already had a drink before I got there and I don't want to switch to wine. What I want is to just get my gin and tonic further on but I don't want people to think I'm an alcoholic and ordering a g and t with dinner but there's no way I'm going to make it through this get-together without drinking and I've only got thirty dollars in my pocket and my credit card has been just-over-the-limit just past the point of good luck. I'm feeling a bit of anxiety. So I drink wine and order the damn spaghetti. It's mostly doctors. A couple other nurses I already know way too well. Somebody from the office. And one doctor brought his friend. A lawyer I think. It's all men. That's okay. I get that. Men like to get together. I mean to homosexual men women are friends and rivals, to heterosexual men women are lovers and enemies. Men are men. And sometimes we like to gather unobserved. Like the animals we are. And if there were women here it would be more social and since it's all men it looks more like a getting together get-together and I'm only here because I want to get together. I haven't been getting together too much since Tee and . . . Truth be told I haven't got anything together since Tee. And it's been a year—a year—I'm ready to get to-get-him, if you know what I mean. But so far it's all kind of formal, almost like it's supposed to be some kind of meeting. Then this doctor starts talking. "We need to form an organization." Oh shit. It *is* a meeting. No wonder there's no women here. The women know what would happen at this meeting. The only place women don't get talked down to and talked over at meetings like this is on TV. But that's why there's

TV. So it turns out I've paid twenty-two dollars for a plate of spaghetti and guaranteed myself a hangover from mixing g and t and wine for a meeting. To form an organization. Now I never liked organizations. The Country Club, that's an organization. The School Board, that's an organization. The Klan. That's an organization. A gay men's organization. Is what he's saying we need to form. And by the looks on a bunch of the faces you can tell this isn't just one person's idea.

Some people are looking at everyone else and not at the person who's talking. Like to say, "What do you think of what *we* thought of?" That's rude. You should always look at the person who's talking. That's just good manners. No matter what you know. And then I'm noticing that everybody kind of has that look on their face. And I'm thinking, "Does everybody else but me know about this?" The doctor speaking, I didn't even know his first name. We're in different areas. I knew his face. Tee used to say a nice ass never hurt a nice face but it sure helped a bad one. Doctor was all right. Doctor All-Right. When Doctor All-Right was talking it was hard to tell if he was the brains or the beauty behind this thing. The only thing I knew for sure about Doctor All-Right was that he was gay. And I don't mean that he was homosexual. I mean he was Gay. Gay is a very specific thing. Gay is a white male who likes the outdoors and chopping vegetables on his granite countertop but isn't afraid to dance on the bar once in a while. He's confident and well-groomed. And somewhere secretly, sometimes deep, deep down and shamefully hidden, he actually kind of gets the Barbra Streisand thing. And he's a lawyer or he's friends with a lawyer or he lives with a lawyer. And he likes sports. Mostly to watch. Baseball, sometimes football. Less often hockey. The uniforms. And he's kind. There's always something impeccable. Impeccable. The house or the accounting or the hair or the smile. And he likes contemporary fiction and architecture and theatre and poetry and anything by Alan Ball. His heroes are David Suzuki and Harvey Milk and occasionally Jesus Christ. He thinks a sense of humour is the most important thing. His religion is most often listed as "other." He drinks socially and he lies about his smoking and he's fit. And seeking same. I am not Gay. And I wouldn't want to be.

No offence. Tee used to say that scorn was just ignorance in a pair of glasses. Just I know Gay. I dated it. It never worked out. There's noting impeccable about me. As Tee would tell you if he could. Now people are talking and nodding. Everybody's agreeing. Talking about *demographics* and *political leverage* and *lobbying* and *exclusivity* but nobody's talking about the thing that's bothering me. Now usually I won't say anything in front of people until after more than one g and t and a glass of wine, but I'm getting bored and I just paid twenty-two dollars for an *okay* plate of spaghetti and nobody's talking about what's bothering me. So I say, "I'm not Gay."

Now things get a little quiet and a couple of the nurses I already know way too well snicker and Doctor All-Right looks at me and says, "So why are you here?" And I say, "Because I'm Queer." Then Doctor All-Right laughs and says something about *semantics* and goes on. He goes on. Just goes on talking like I didn't say anything, or like what I said didn't mean anything. But I can see a couple of people are looking at me like they might agree. So I say it again, louder, "I'm not Gay." How these things happen I'm not quite sure. It's like there are teams and all of a sudden you're playing this game you didn't know you were playing and halfway through the game you're made captain. I don't know. All I'm really seeing is Doctor All-Right and his impeccable hair and his impeccable smile and his impeccable shirt. And he says something and I stand up. That's what they told me. I thought he stood up first. It felt like he stood up—I remember it as he stood up. But recounted to me: I stood up after what he said. "Is this about race?" And it wasn't till then I noticed how white the table was. Just a Japanese doctor and a nurse from the Philippines. "Is this about race?" Yes it most certainly is because we're talking about North America here. And I've been a North American for hundreds of years. My family worked and died here for generations. Is this about race? It's sure as hell about *a* race. Yes it's a damn race. Maybe not at your dinner tables or in your parking lots and your hospitals.

But out there in the newspapers and in magazines and on the flat screens it's a race with no finish line. Is Asia one country? Does Ireland come with name tags? And I tell him so. I tell him about the race he's in and he doesn't even know. And first thing he does is get apologetic. And that does nothing but exacerbate the breakout.

And when I don't accept his apology he talks about "dialogue." I hate "dialogue." "Dialogue" is just one person talking and one person sitting on their hands. And I tell him so and he stands up. That's when he stood up. And that's when I was moving. I was headed for his chair. And some voice at the table says, "Hey there, you!" Not "hey fill-in-my-name" or just "hey" or even "hey there" but, "Hey there, you!" Hey there you who I don't know and don't want to know and is a troublemaker who doesn't belong here, doesn't fit here, only has thirty dollars in his pocket and two hundred to his name and will never own a house and can't keep one good man alive—hey there, you—you who isn't me and will never be.

He looks off toward the dog.

When Tee died it felt like it was my fault. I quit smoking. And when I did smoke I never smoked in the house. But it felt like my fault because my job is to save lives. But I couldn't. No one could. I heard a story once; it was on a video on the Internet. It was a dog hit by a car on a highway and another dog, his buddy, trying to drag him through the traffic to the other side, to safety. The video ended before you found out what happened. Some people say the dog made it. I think he didn't.

A moment.

I *know* it's not my fault but it doesn't stop it from *feeling* that way.

A moment.

"Hey there, you." And it was like those words pushed a button that tightened a band that turned a gear that lifted my arm. How did that happen? Who did that?

Was that me?

It wasn't a punch. It was more of a smash. A slap. A man slap. A man slap like my old man hit me. No shoulder in it. All from the elbow. But if you're not ready for it it can put you back, take your feet out, find the floor with your ass. I hit Tee like that once. He hit me back harder. We never had to have the conversation again.

He looks off.

I don't know what love is but I know that it's fatal. Somebody understands you so much you feel like you're going to disappear. And maybe that's the feeling people want. Maybe it's supposed to feel that strange and that scary. Love feels like a bit of a cult to me. Of course I could be wrong.

How come on TV when somebody dies everything gets better? Everything goes on. People cry and then later it's okay. Is it just not like that or is it just me?

I never hit anyone but Tee before. But when I hit Tee I was hitting myself. I've threatened to hit someone before, when necessary. I've made a face like I could hit somebody. And I've run. I've run a lot. Doctor All-Right ran. I didn't expect him to run. But I knew he wouldn't fight back. Gay guys don't fight back. I mean they do with words or ideas or lawyers, but not with fists. They realize how pointless it is. Especially after all that dental work.

I prefer "Queer." It sounds like something anyone could be. Queer is deeper than personality. Don't tell me what I am. Don't tell me what I am until you've at least given me a chance to figure it out myself. When Tee died I got Larry. He's a good dog. And he doesn't complain about what I watch on TV and he doesn't cook. Which is a good thing if you know Tee. If you knew Tee.

People cross lines. People cross lines all the time. But sometimes people cross lines they don't know are there. Sometimes you have to be on a certain side of the line to see the line. My mother used to say "if you cross the line it disappears." But I guess you've got to know it's there, and I guess you've got to want it to disappear. And this morning I woke up feeling boxed in by lines. There was no way out of my head. So I made the call. And you know, I thought, in the back of my head, looking for the phone, dialling the number, people meet like this. On TV. In movies. It happens all the time. An argument, a fight. A doctor and a nurse. An apology. A coffee shop. A kiss. A new condo with a big kitchen. Vacations at a cottage on a lake. Two dogs.

Doctor All-Right took the call. Confident. Impeccable. Kind. But he only took the call to say he couldn't take the call. To say we can't behave like animals. *We aren't animals.* To say his lawyer would be in touch with me. To talk about a broken tooth and the principle. The *principal. The principal will see you now.*

A dog whimpers.

(off) Larry, no! Sorry about that, sir. He's just a dog. He's a dog's dog, he is. An animal.

He looks up.

(to us) Look at that moon.

He howls.

Boy In Hoodie

Outside. Night. A neighbourhood.

A teenaged boy in a hoodie holds a flashlight to his face.

The moon is dead. Dead. Dead. Die. Death. Death. Comes. Not. Death comes not because death is already here. Death lives. Life is Death.

He drops the flashlight to his side.

"Life Is Death." As a band. Excellent band name. Everything. Protons and neutrons and subatomic particles. A grain of sand on a beach on a particle the size of a grain of sand on a beach on a particle the size of a grain of sand. Times infinity.

Constantly in motion. Without movement there is nothing. But that's not death. Death is different than nothing. Those protons and neutrons and subatomic particles don't die. They just are or are not. Only ideas die. And thoughts die. And bodies die. But ideas are made of thoughts and bodies are made of thoughts. Bodies are just something to think about. Bodies are the transformers of thought. Bodies are just something to walk around in and pick things up with. Bodies die. Thoughts die. But the protons and neutrons and subatomic particles are infinite. Unless they're not. Then they're just not. Into infinity. "Into Infinity." Good band name.

I'm standing in Beverly Fitzgerald's driveway. It's Saturday night and I'm standing in Beverly Fitzgerald's driveway. I don't know that it's Beverly Fitzgerald's driveway. Or I don't think I know it's Beverly Fitzgerald's driveway. And I'm standing there looking at the moon.

He looks up.

People can make spaceships out of energy fields around their bodies and travel to other planets. Other dimensions. That's fucked up. I wouldn't do it. What if you got stuck there? What if it was worse than here? The moon is a good thing though.

Without the moon there would be no tides, no midnight. The moon keeps things interesting.

He looks to us.

I should never have asked for that telescope for my birthday. They took away my camera so I asked for a telescope. I got in trouble for looking at things I could see so I thought it would be safer to look at things I couldn't see. And now because I asked for a telescope I'm supposed to be good at math. I guess because people who want telescopes are secretly good at math. People who are bad at math are supposedly good at math but get taught math wrong. So now because I asked for a telescope I have to take these stupid extra classes after freaking school with a tutor who teaches this math for people who are bad at math because they don't know they're good at math. What about for people who just *don't like* math? Maybe I'm bad at math because I don't like math. Maybe I just wanted a telescope and it has nothing to do with math. I should have asked for a laptop.

A moment.

My mom said that when she was in school sometimes the teacher would play records. In class. She played me one. Cat Stevens. That's fucked up. You couldn't do that now. There'd be a riot. It would be on the news.

He looks up.

You know at 9/11 within one hour of the planes they had a theme song for it. I remember even though I was really little. I was watching TV. I remember the music. I think that's the first thing I remember. My first memory. That music. And the pictures of the screen. My second memory is when my father died.

He looks to us.

"I have some bad news." I remember that being said. My mother said that. "I have some bad news." That's the first time anybody ever said that to me. Or maybe when I was a baby and I don't remember somebody might have. But why would somebody say "I have some bad news" to a baby. "I have some bad news." Nobody ever says "I have some bad news" unless they really do. But it's all bad news.

Everything is bad news. Life is bad news. Unless "we are made of thought and thought dies" is good news to you. And if it is good news to you, then think of me next time you're dancing with a fairy in a field under a rainbow. Dancing with a fairy in a field under a rainbow. That would suck as a band name. That band would suck. Or it would be brilliant. Ed has a rainbow on a T-shirt. A rainbow in his brain. You know, dream catchers and pot and a ponytail, a rainbow in his brain. My mom's been trying to get him to cut his ponytail for years. It's not even a ponytail now. It's more like a skinny grey tail now. It's okay to me but kind of depressing. Getting old.

Shrinking. Turning to dust. He never asked me to call him Dad. I appreciated that. My mom was always, "You can call him Dad if you want to." And this is way after the best-before date for that conversation. Ed doesn't care. We don't need to have that conversation. Ed and me have lots of *conversations*. Especially lately. That's what Ed calls it, "a *conversation*." And you can tell the difference between when he says "a conversation" when he means talking to some neighbour about politics or when he says "a *conversation*" when he means smoking a fatty. Ed says there's nothing wrong with pot. My mom doesn't really agree. She would freak if she knew Ed was having *conversations* with me. But he doesn't tell her. I appreciate that.

He looks up.

And I'm standing in Beverly Fitzgerald's driveway and I'm laughing because I'm thinking about something Ed said, and I hear, "What's so funny?" And that's one of those really hard questions, like, "What are you thinking." Actually it's even harder than "what are you thinking" because whatever you're thinking had better be funny if you have to tell somebody. And it's especially hard because you didn't know anyone could hear you, and that is more especially hard because as soon as you realize someone could hear you you immediately forget what you laughed at, and most especially it's a hard question because Beverly Fitzgerald is asking it. And this when I realize that the driveway I'm standing in is Beverly Fitzgerald's driveway.

And this is when I realize that Beverly Fitzgerald is sitting in the dark on her front step. How long has she been there?

(to her) Oh hey. What's so funny? Just life, you know; the joke of life, you know. We are puppets; we are sheep, as the Down say.

Oh yeah? Really?

(to us) She loves the Down? Beverly Fitzgerald loves the Down? Beverly Fitzgerald is a cheerleader. Beverly Fitzgerald is a

cheerleader who goes to church. The Down is the music you put on when you want your best friend from grade seven who turned out to be really creepy to go home. The Down is the only music your mom yells "turn that down" at. Even Ed. At first he was all "whatever" but one time he came into my room and he says, "How can that music be in any way helpful?" Helpful? I'm not looking for *help*. If I was looking for help I'd call the Youth Distress Line. I'm not looking for help; I'm looking for confirmation. I mean Ed might have a rainbow in his brain but he knows that we are made of thought and thought dies. He agreed. I remind him. But then he starts talking about trees and eagles and bears and that's when I turn up the Down. Confirmation.

Beverly Fitzgerald loves the Down. If Beverly Fitzgerald were a time of day she would be morning in the summer before anyone is up. If she were a drink she'd be that lemon water my mom makes by putting just lemon slices in water in a glass pitcher and stirring it with a glass wand that makes that sound when you stir it, the sound of the taste of the lemon. If she were a colour she would be yellow. If she were a band she would not be the Down. Beverly Fitzgerald is a cheerleader.

Beverly Fitzgerald goes to church. I went to church once and my mom had a fit. I only went because there was a party after. But it turned out it was just a bunch of priests trying to start a cult or something. And all the other kids smoked. It was worse than just a normal crappy Sunday afternoon. Beverly

Fitzgerald goes out with a college guy. Beverly Fitzgerald is popular. Nobody popular likes the Down.

A moment.

When I was popular I didn't know what popular was. It just happened by accident. First there was just a gang of us from the neighbourhood who would hang out and then the gang starts to split up into two or three gangs and it's like you've got to decide which mini gang you're going to hang with and so you do and then it's just kind of by accident that one part of the gang get's popular and one part of the gang gets weird and one part of the gang starts to smoke meth. I got popular by accident. Mostly you have to be looking for the popular people to get popular. I wasn't. I was just following Gerry. But Gerry was looking for the popular people. That sucked. I didn't know I was popular until we kept ending up at pool parties at houses with gardeners and liquor cabinets and all this popularness and I told Gerry I thought these people kind of sucked and he said but they were *his people.* That sucked. Gerry hated the Down. Gerry would love Beverly though. He would say she was a boneless starlet. *(laughs)* "What's the special tonight? Boneless starlet." *(laughs)* Like in a restaurant. She could be on TV. She's got a website. But it doesn't say she loves the Down on her website. It's just shit about what she does and opinions and stuff. I mean apparently. Or whatever. I had a website. It was pictures of cats. Not cute cats or stupid dressed-up cats or anything. One time there was this site of cats with stuff on them? Just random stuff. It was hilarious. So I started taking pictures of my cat with like a phone on him or a slipper or a mug. The mug was hilarious. The cat was asleep. And then I just started taking pictures of my cat. And then other cats. Not doing anything special. Not knowing I was there. Just being cats. Sleeping or eating or watching TV. My cat watches TV. And one time just that second after the cat saw a mouse. Not my cat. Some random cat. They're pretty good. I like cats. I get cats. I used to dream sometimes that I was a cat. Cats don't take anything from anybody. They're on their own and okay with that. I took lots of pictures of lots of cats.

A moment.

And one time a picture of a dead cat. It was just some random dead cat. He was hit by a car. It was just a picture. It was a huge deal. It was on the news. I had to change schools. And which, why is that better? At least at my old school people knew me. First day at the new school I'm the Dead Cat Kid that nobody knows.

Good luck with that. Gerry wouldn't even look at me. After it kind of blew over I walked by his place. He was out shooting hoops with his brother. It was "Hey," "Hey," and I shot a few. Then Gerry goes inside and I think for his phone or a whiz or whatever. So I keep shooting hoops with his brother. And Gerry doesn't come back. He wouldn't even look at me. That was embarrassing. That sucked. And it turns out it wasn't even his choice to dis me. It was one of these new friends of

24

his whose mother was the fucking city planner or some shit. Gerry's brother told me. She said I was a dark influence. "Dark Influence." Good band name. So just like that I'm cut off. That was cold.

He looks up for a moment.

So I go to this new school. Ed bought me one of those New York Fire Department "stay-back-500-feet" T-shirts to wear. That was funny. But I never wore it. At first people were just scared. Then people got curious. The assholes got curious first. They'd get drunk and yell questions that are supposed to be funny in rooms full of people. Then the really creepy people started coming around. But they have *true* creepiness radar and they can tell when somebody is a cat killer or somebody just took a picture of an already dead cat. So they just crawled back under the bleachers. Then the more-normal people. The more-normal people can be good at seeming like everything's cool. They started out with talking about music or having a laugh and then a conversation. But they really just wanted answers to questions. To report back to the group. They want the story. The Story of the Dead Cat Kid. *(laughs)* That's the new album from Dark Influence. Drops this Christmas. Walmarts worldwide. *(laughs)* And I'm the Dead Cat Kid and I don't know anyone and I'm at some stupid assembly on hand-washing or gun violence or some useless thing. If you're interested in not spreading a virus or not having a riot, don't have an assembly. And this girl gets up to thank the doctor or the cop for speaking and they say her name. Beverly

Fitzgerald. And I think of Gerry because he would have loved that, "Beverly Fits Me!" Nobody but his gramma called him Gerald but it still would've worked. Beverly Fits Gerald. He would have loved that. And I actually cracked a smile and I remember I did because it was the first time I think I smiled since I got to that school. Like I'm supposed to be in mourning all my life now. It was just a picture. And there's Beverly Fitzgerald and she's thanking the cop or the doctor and she's like a movie star. She's like a woman. I could see her in *Maxim*.

Yesterday. And apparently she's in some science club but she likes to party on weekends. And she's got a car. She's perfect. And I'm the Dead Cat Kid and I'm standing in Beverly Fitzgerald's driveway and I just found out she loves the Down and that her parents are away. And she invites me inside.

He looks up for a moment.

My parents never go away. Ed and my mom never go away. Nobody I know's parents ever go away. Beverly Fitzgerald's life is like a TV show. My mother won't have a TV in the house. She calls it emotional pornography. She doesn't say that to me. That's what she tells Ed.

He plays with the flashlight a moment.

When Beverly Fitzgerald said "wanna come in?" I knew that's what she said but I couldn't believe that's what she said. Maybe she said "water the grass," which some people do at night, or maybe she said "gonna kick it," which maybe could mean take off or disappear. So I didn't say anything and she had to say it again. And I didn't say "yes" or anything. I just went in. All the lights were on. Ed would freak. Before he goes to bed Ed *unplugs* everything! There was a funny little chair in the living room. It was like made by a farmer or something. You couldn't sit on it. It had birds and shit painted on it like a kid did it. All red and blue and yellow and stuff. It was something like Ed might like. But everything else was white. My mom would freak. She says white is the absence of colour; she hates white. To my mom hell would be white. White hell. It looked cool though. Expensive like in a magazine. White sofa, white-like carpets, white chairs in the dining room. Metal chairs in the kitchen.

Beverly Fitzgerald gets me a beer from her fridge. I just put it on the counter. I don't drink. My mom would freak. Plus I don't really like it. It makes me sleepy. Beverly Fitzgerald likes her vodka though. Beverly Fitzgerald's drinking vodka. Her phone is always ringing but she doesn't answer it. Texts keep coming in so she turns it off. She might be drunker than she looks. She's pretty funny. Talking smack about everybody, and herself. She was pretty funny. And I ask her if she wants to *have a conversation* and she doesn't know what that means. So I explain to her that having a *conversation* is smoking a fatty. I guess it's just Ed's thing. I thought it was, you know, synonymous. So she really gets excited and she turns off all the lights and makes us go to the basement, which is like a lounge in an airport, with a bar. So we *have a conversation*, but I can tell why she doesn't call it *having a conversation* because as soon as she has two puffs she gets really quiet. At first. Just mostly looking at her hands. But then she started talking. But it wasn't a conversation. This long story about some party she didn't go to tonight. And then she wanted to put on some music. I said the Down and she got excited and had to go upstairs to get it.

And I'm in Beverly Fitzgerald's downstairs airport lounge bar and her parents are away and she's maybe more that a little bit drunk and we just had a *conversation* and she just went upstairs to get the Down. And I feel like this: *Phew.* That's the perfect word for the sound because the sound is the word and the feeling all together: *Phew.* Everything's going to be okay. Things are going to get normal finally. Things are going to get better than normal. And Beverly Fitzgerald comes back from upstairs and puts on the Down and she dances to it. I've never seen anyone dance to the Down before. Like this angry ballet. Like they dance on TV. She could be on TV. And then some other music comes on and I don't remember what because while Beverly Fitzgerald was dancing to the Down I had a *conversation* with myself. Hook-up music I think. And Beverly Fitzgerald starts taking off her clothes. Her shirt and her bra. She fell down taking off her pants. She was laughing.

He turns the flashlight on and off, playing with it. He holds it briefly in his face.

It's just protons and neutrons and strings of DNA. It's the nothing of everything; it's the end of thought. But in the middle of all the ending and the nothing is an eye and in the centre of the eye is a tiny iris. And inside the iris is a garden.

He turns the flashlight off.

The flashlight is for cats. You go out at night and sneak up on them and you take the picture at the same time you turn on the flashlight. They always look like they've been up to something. Like they've been caught. I don't have my camera anymore but I still just like to look at the cats.

A moment.

After we did it Beverly Fitzgerald threw up and turned her phone back on. She stayed in the bathroom for a long time. When she came out she had another vodka. She talked about the party again and answered the phone a bunch of times. It seemed like she wanted me to leave a couple of times, and after about three I got up to go and she walked me to the door. And we were at the door and I turned to her 'cause I'm not sure to kiss her or hug her or shake hands and she says, "Did you kill the cat?"

He turns on the flashlight.

I was just coming round the corner. And I had the flashlight on. Watching my feet on the sidewalk. Sometimes taking pictures of my feet on the sidewalk. And I stop and I see this thing on the road. And it's a cat and it's dead. It must have been hit by a car but there's no blood and nothing flattened. It's just like a normal looking cat lying down on the road, but he's dead. And you can tell he's dead. And the only way to tell that he's dead is not by something that's there—guts or crushed bones—but by what's not there. And I stood there for a long time looking at the cat and I thought, "I am the cat." I am the cat. We are the cat. We are all the cat. And it was like I was trying to send what was alive in me into the cat and if I could do that it would wake up, stand up, take off, fly away. Send my thoughts into the cat. But I couldn't. Do cats think? What dies in a cat when a cat dies? Then I moved him to the sidewalk. That's when I touched him. He was heavy. I didn't kill him. It was just a picture.

He turns off the flashlight.

And Beverly Fitzgerald says, "Did you kill the cat?" and I say yes.

He looks up.

Ed says "people see what they see; you can only be responsible for what you do." But I say you can be responsible for what they see. Depending on what you show them, depending on the story you tell.

He looks at us.

Ed liked the picture. Not like he *liked* it, but he got it. It wasn't his favourite. He likes a lot of them. He showed them to some friend of his who knows about that shit and he said they were pretty good. They're pretty good. "Pretty good." But it's the end of the world, and we are puppets; we are sheep, and government is religion, and God is physics and Nature is dying and what difference does "pretty good" make? Even if "great." What difference does "great" make if there's no future anyway?

He looks up.

Yeah yeah, get me the Youth Distress Line please, it's an emergency. It's all good. I can talk to Ed. We'll have a *conversation* about it. Don't tell my mom. She would freak.

My mom hated that picture. She hated it more than anybody. It's just a picture. Pixilations of pixilations. There's nothing there.

He looks at us.

And right now Beverly Fitzgerald is on the phone or at a party and she's telling everyone she talks to and everyone who wants to talk to her what the Dead Cat Kid said.

Monday will be interesting at school.

"Monday Will Be Interesting." Could work. For a band.

He holds the flashlight in his face and speaks in a scary voice.

Ladies and gentlemen, put your hands together for Monday Will Be Interesting!

I could always just move.

He looks up at the moon.

He reaches up to touch the moon.

To the moon.

Woman In Prada

Outside an airport. Night.

A well-dressed woman sits on a bench next to her suitcases talking on her phone.

(on phone) I'm not talking to you, Jean-Marc . . . I'm not talking to you, Jean-Marc . . . I'm at the airport . . . At the airport . . . Which airport? This airport. *Here* of course. I only left the resort an hour ago, have a thought in your head, Jean-Marc. I'd have to travel on a *spaceship* to be at an airport other than *here* . . . Outside the airport . . . On a bench . . . No I'm not smoking . . . Well I don't know how you're going to do that, Jean-Marc . . . Well good luck coming to get me, Jean-Marc, because I took the rental . . . I took the car . . . I returned it. So I don't know how you're going to come and get me because you can't afford a cab and the bus will take far too long . . . I took the credit card . . . I checked out . . . Your plane ticket for Tuesday is in the desk drawer . . . Do what you want . . .

"How are you going to get to the airport on Tuesday?" Is that what you're asking me? Ask *Connie*!

She hangs up, angry.

She takes a pill from her bag and swallows it with water from a bottle she carries.

Aspirin. Never take anything else on a hangover. The rest damages your liver. You notice how Aspirin is everywhere again? Maybe there are more hangovers these days. There are for me. And more airports. It's actually the best place to have a hangover. You can wear your pyjamas and eat pizza and sleep on the floor. Not that I've ever worn my pyjamas in public. Maybe if Prada made pyjamas. Not that I've ever slept on an airport floor. But it's nice to know it's an option. Take a swim in the river of humanity. All equal in transport. All of us trusting a perplexing science and an aging technology with our lives. All because we're not where we want to be. Or perhaps it's less about *wanting* be anywhere and more about wanting to be anywhere but *here*. Leaving. Leaving abruptly. Leaving abruptly is not new for me. International *and* domestic. Oh not always in a flare of fireworks—it can be, but often it's just at a party and I'm chatting and suddenly I'm home and the people I went to the party with are wondering if I want another drink. I'm not much for goodbye. Hello has always been my strong suit.

Connie and the Redhead and Jean-Marc and me. For two weeks. On a beach. In adjoining villas. What was I *thinking*?

Maybe I was hoping this would happen. This was my plan? Next time I make a plan like this I'm going to need sponsors, put a logo on my luggage, it's very expensive. Jean-Marc is one of those men, unlike my husband, who has none of his masculine self-image tied up in the handling, spending or receiving of money. Which initially was a relief but has become something of a yoke. Or more like a bridle. A bridle that he's wearing but doesn't see, and I'm left holding the reins. And to no effect since how can you actually ride the horse if the horse doesn't know he's being ridden. Or doesn't care. And he at his age and me at mine you can't help but start to *hear* what people *see*. They don't have to say a thing; the judgment is loud and clear in their eyes. And what the hell can I do about that? I hate that I care. But when someone actually says it. Someone you've known.

Someone your age. And maybe to their own designs.

The phone rings. She answers it.

What? . . . I told you . . . It's on the ticket . . . Tuesday . . . The day after tomorrow . . . I don't know. Stay with Connie . . . Stay with Connie and the Redhead . . . That's not my problem . . . I don't know . . . I don't know . . . Look, just to get you off the phone I'll call the hotel and approve another night. Don't call back.

She hangs up.

Apparently no one is speaking now. And I am delighted. And what of that? That's what Love looks like without its makeup first thing in the morning. That wasn't always my notion of Love. Let's just say reality has transformed that notion. What it looks like. What it feels like. I had always believed that it was out there. To be claimed. And then people started talking about the *work* of it. And then you find out what that meant. And there are payoffs—small, profound payoffs. And so you start working for the payoffs. But as any nine-to-fiver will tell you, when you start only working for the weekends they get shorter and farther away and they end up buckling under expectation. And then that odd expression you always felt was just a tad too dark, a bit *mean*—"familiarity breeds contempt"— becomes so benign and practical, so *obvious*. And contempt is sticky, like Velcro in a clothes dryer. And it can attach to every statement, every gesture, every open-mouthed meal. Ah the table. At table with a lover. Revolting.

I have issues at the table. That's how I was raised. It's an intimate exchange. It requires ritual. Diplomacy. My father ran dinner like a meting of nations. Knives have a purpose and elbows have their place. And for god's sake close your bloody mouth when you chew. Jean-Marc is fourteen. My husband is eighty-four. Neither literally. But in truth Jean-Marc is closer to fourteen as my husband is to eighty-four. That reality is rather chilling. But isn't that what they told us years ago? Back before we thought we'd care? A woman in her prime and a man in his prime. That's a vast difference. That was how biology had wanted it. Now it's cougars and MILFs. How suburban.

I take no mortal offence with the suburbs, I have grown to accept their necessity, but I was always in my heart a city girl. My parents lived in the city before the city was convenient. You didn't raise children in the city when I was raised in the city. There were other city dwellers but they were all about boarding schools and summer homes. Rural weekends and exhausted, anonymous weeknights. We grew up in a two-storey pre-war flat and crumbing city schools and difficult art galleries and standing-room only buses and family-run Italian restaurants for dinner and the perfect chaos of finding a cab downtown at ten past five with three children and shopping. I never believed I'd end up in the suburbs. But a person can get used to anything. Suddenly there are children. I don't know how my parents did it. With the option of yards and corner lots and children safely in the street or next door or around the block. I had no choice. And there were payoffs. Long, quiet days of solitude. Long lunches at the golf club. Unexpected friendships. Gathering in a storm. The stables close by. There is nothing, nothing, nothing in the world like a horse. Riding is an affectation only to those who don't ride. A horse is a thing to know. An understanding of the world. A horse is not controlled; a horse allows himself to be controlled. The noblest beast. And the moment of understanding the nobility of that dance with control is the point when little girls either become young women who ride or remain girls who dream of horses. To be offered that power by an animal, over an animal, who so easily could control you. Always trust. Occasionally fear. But what is trust? More and more people are being led to believe that trust involves some kind of truth. But no. It involves honesty, not truth. A horse understands the difference between the truth and honesty. The truth is very noisy. Honesty is silent. The absence of truth is simply a lie; the absence of honesty is fear. And what is fear? I should be able to define it since I feel it so deeply.

Secretly. Shh. Although it seems to have thinned out to anxiety now. A buzzing anxiety. Like I'm holding live batteries in wet hands, and carrying a spare set in my bag. Perhaps it's what keeps me going. Because I *do* keep on going. Like that thing with the pink bunny. Going going going. Gone. I'm not yet though. But much is.

The husband. The security of schedule. The children.

My children grew up and became a doctor and a lesbian. We've had both in the family before. Of some prominence. My aunt is an important lesbian professor at an important university. My father was a GP then a surgeon then a GP again. And that came in very handy when trying to hide a pregnancy. Ancient tales those. And on that topic, the lesbian doesn't want children and the doctor says she doesn't either so I'm off the hook. No grandmother for me. Rah rah. Sometimes after the third of a two-martini lunch a girlfriend will say how I must be sad. And usually I give them a moment or two of that. Mostly for their benefit. For the benefit of avoiding an uncomfortable moment. Me laughing, martini sloshing, "Hell no!" And I'm mostly not sad for having avoided the rift. The inevitable *rift*. A mother has a daughter, there's all of that. But a daughter has a child.

And there's the mother and the daughter and the child. That can go off in all kinds of unpleasant, uncomfortable directions. I've seen it with my friends. Staking territory. Fixing mistakes.

Resenting. Revenging. Apologizing. And none of those qualities hold their liquor very well. Or dress very well. Following fashion falls behind when you're on a mission.

I've always dressed well. We were *dressed*. Mother had us *dressed*. Not outfitted, not supplied, but *dressed*. As children, and especially as teenagers, we balked and pulled at the reins but now I'm thankful. It's how I've filled my time. I dress people. I talk on television about fashion. On afternoon shows for women. I have lunch with a girl and we go shopping and then I go on TV and talk about the clothes. You may have seen me if you're home that time of day with the television on. If you are one of the many who understand that kind of low-level inertia. I had a shop. To have kept it open would have only served vanity, not accounts. I don't need money though. I suppose if I started buying yachts and baseball teams and cocaine I'd start needing money. But I just buy luggage and shoes. And jewellery. I don't need anybody's money. My father saw to that. His motto was: "Money, make it to keep it." It was my mother's money but my father's to spend; my father's to control. My mother was a horse. Giving control. Noble to a fault. A palomino. Not just her golden skin and white blond hair. Did you know that all the actor horses were palominos? The smart horses. Trigger. Mister Ed. Poor Mister Ed. Apparently they pulled his lips with a wire. But he let them.

My mother was a wonderful grandmother. Born to be a grandmother. She had to become a grandmother to become a good mother. That was nice. I was a good mother. Ask the lesbian. I told her she was a lesbian before she told me. And she denied it for a year. But I kept encouraging. Is that shocking? People often say I'm shocking. I don't feel shocking. I think perhaps I'm missing a filter. My husband started to find me shocking. I think he just got boring.

When he told me he was leaving, I was fine with it. Our lives had grown more solitary. I assumed there would be a simple arrangement. There was a silly girl. A silly girl. All hair and nipples. And there was nothing *real* about it all at first, just silly. Silly her. And him, how foolish he looked. He was five years too old for a mid-life crisis—this was delusional. And then something got real. The silly girl got greedy. So a shiny-headed lawyer and a messy divorce and all sorts of unnecessary social unpleasantness. And as the bile churned it was Me the Fool. For having thought I'd *known* this man. For having *loved* this man. At least loved him in the eyes of our world of Nembutal dinner parties and charity golf tournaments and Juvéderm parties. That's still love. Perhaps that's real love, being *seen* as having loved. From the outside. But then the inside came out. Then I wasn't so fine. And I told everyone who would listen. Not just what happened but how I felt. No diplomacy, no etiquette, no discretion. And I may very well have indicated socially one lubricated evening that the silly girl with the nipples was a prostitute—and that was very possibly the very words I used—the fact that I don't remember has no bearing on whether or not it was said. Be warned, blackout drinking is best done out of the public eye and when one *is* in public benign euphemisms are essential in avoiding a lawsuit. Nipples is suing me. She probably just found out all the money is mine.

She takes out her phone and dials.

I don't resent paying Jean-Marc's way as much as I resent people knowing. People's opinions. People's assumptions.

(on phone) I'd like to rebook Villa Three for one more night . . . Oh really? . . . Who checked out?

. . . The younger gentleman? . . . I see . . . Did he say— Oh never mind . . . Pardon me? . . . Well why would I need the villa when the occupant has checked out? . . . That's right.

. . . *Au revoir.*

She hangs up the phone.

There's a wonderful word. Gobsmacked. Stricken to silence. That's a perfect way to describe it. Hit in the face. Not *being* hit in the face but *having been* hit in the face. The silent moment after, before the reactions, the retractions, the retaliations, the protections. Everything stopping in recognition of what just happened. I was gobsmacked.

The Redhead was down at the beach and Jean-Marc was napping and Connie and I were playing backgammon and having a cocktail on the patio. Connie is eight years younger but years of sun damage levels us out. We hadn't been quite *with it* all day; it had been a night the night before. And Jean-Marc stumbles out onto the patio half asleep and he's not dressed. He always walks around like that at home. He can get away with it. And he picks up his cigarettes and he looks over to say something to me and he sees that Connie is there. And I think he gets embarrassed for a second. Which is very sweet. He seldom embarrasses. And his embarrassment embarrasses him but he refuses to admit it, so he stands there chatting. It's deliciously uncomfortable, achingly charming. And Jean-Marc goes back into the villa and I'm a bit aglow—a lovely moment, his beauty, his sweetness, his blush, and I'm thinking Connie is probably envious of all this. Her and her Redhead, him being so thick and dull and usually pickled, she found somewhere we've never discussed, and it's clear even now that he will prove to be so insignificant in her eventual story. And I get a feeling like smug. A warm little smug. And I look at Connie, there still smiling, still watching off after little Prince Jean-Marc. And after too long a wait and too held a smile she looks at me and hushed and serious says "I'm your friend." Why didn't this give me pause? Prepare me? Brace me? But it was that warm smiling little smug, sitting on my shoulders like a stole. I was unprepared. "I'm your friend so I need to tell you. He makes you look foolish."

We'd had this conversation before. Many times. After a strange evening or a teary lunch I'd ask Connie if I looked foolish. She

42

always said no. And I made her promise to tell me if that ever became the case. "If you're my friend," I said. I thought I'd react better. Although I don't imagine I ever believed I'd hear it from her. I said nothing.

For the rest of the afternoon. Connie tried to reapproach the subject several times but eventually found her own angry silence. She went to the beach to find the Redhead. Jean-Marc was still asleep. I packed my bags and left. I hate that I care.

She puts the phone away.

I don't know where I'm going. I don't want to go home. I could take a few days with friends in Nova Scotia. Key West. Galiano. Do a survey. "How foolish on a scale of one to ten?"

She's jealous. When I told her I was going to cut my hair and she said it wouldn't suit me—but it did, by many accounts it did, and never did she say it did. That's not taste; it's tenacity. Undermining my daughters' choices with "it must be sad."

Spending my money. I understand resentment. It comes up; you face it; you let it go. But this is too much. This is beyond. This is betrayal. My daughters would have told me. Honestly. My daughters would know. My daughters would have told me. I hate that I care.

I don't feel old. But I feel things that I didn't feel before. I am aware of the humanity of things. My knees. My heart once.

My fingers more and more. My eyes long ago and slowly my hearing. But I don't feel old. And despite my knees and my fingers and my ears I look pretty good.

I hate that I care. I wish I still had horses. They didn't care of such things. They ran until they couldn't run anymore but they didn't long for what they no longer had.

They didn't know what was lost. They only knew this. This now. Here this now. A horse would remind me. A horse would. Something lean and quiet, fast. Something here and this and now.

Jean-Marc is not that young. He's older than he looks. He's getting a belly. I like it. He doesn't. On the patio today he was only concerned about hiding his belly. And if I am a fool, so what? Where's he going to go? Connie? I wouldn't be surprised. The Readhead doesn't even have a last name yet. Connie's always had an eye for Jean-Marc. She very well might.

I hate that I think she might. I hate how foolish that makes me look.

I don't know where I'm going. I've got great luggage and a plane ticket and everywhere to possibly go. But I don't know where to go. And in some ways that scares me and in some ways that makes me feel like a fourteen-year-old girl who just fell in love with a horse and there's a boy I maybe like and my dreams will all come true.

And in some ways it scares me.

She looks up.

Look at that moon.

I can be amazed. I can look up and be amazed. Amazed that I'm still here. Amazed that it's still happening. Amazed that I can still be amazed. Amazed at the intricate unending patterns of stars. At the moon.

Speaking of amazing? This on-board bag? Spins, swivels, expands. Fine engineering. Not unlike myself.

I don't know where I'm going.

The phone rings. She answers it.

I said don't call back . . . Did you check out? . . . What? . . . You said that to whom? . . . *(laughing)* Jean-Marc, that's terrible . . . Well what did Connie say to that? . . . *(laughing)* That's terrible . . . Where? Here? . . . How long? . . . I'll meet you at Departures B . . . I'm outside at B . . . Why would we stay in the airport hotel? . . . No, Jean-Marc, we don't wait for the flight, we change it, have a thought in your head . . . Listen, I think I left my silver bracelet in the— Thank you . . . I'll see you at B.

She hangs up. She looks up.

It's not too late to get a horse.

Light fades.

End.

Daniel MacIvor is one of Canada's most accomplished playwrights and performers. Winner of the prestigious Elinore and Lou Siminovitch Prize, a GLAAD Award, the Governor General's Literary Award, and many others, Daniel's plays have been met with acclaim throughout North America.

First edition: May 2015

Printed and bound in Canada by Imprimerie Gauvin, Gatineau

Cover and book design by Blake Sproule
Author photo © Guntar Kravis

 PLAYWRIGHTS CANADA PRESS

202-269 Richmond St. W.
Toronto, ON
M5V 1X1

416.703.0013
info@playwrightscanada.com
playwrightscanada.com